A Read-Together Book for Parents & Children ™

Sometimes I Get Angry

by Jane Werner Watson

Robert E. Switzer, M.D.
Former Director of the Children's Division
The Menninger Clinic

J. Cotter Hirschberg, M.D.
William C. Menninger Distinguished Professor of Psychiatry
The Menninger Clinic

with pictures by Irene Trivas

Crown Publishers, Inc.   New York

A Read-Together Book for Parents and Children™
Created in cooperation with The Menninger Foundation

The Dorothy Wright Treatment and Endowment Fund defrays a part of the care
and treatment cost at the Children's Division
of the Menninger Clinic, Box 829, Topeka, Kansas 66601.
Part of the income from the sale of this book goes to that fund.

Library of Congress Cataloging-in-Publication Data. Watson, Jane Werner, 1915–   Sometimes I get angry. (A Read-together book for parents and children) Summary: A little boy describes some of the things that make him angry and what he does about it. 1. Anger—Juvenile·literature. [1. Anger] I. Switzer, Robert E., 1918–   . II. Hirschberg, J. Cotter, 1915–   . III. Trivas, Irene, ill. IV. Title. V. Series. BF723.A4W38   1986   155.4′23   85-24246
ISBN 0-517-56088-7
10 9 8 7 6 5 4 3 2 1
First Edition

NOTE TO PARENTS

It would be great if the process of a child's growth and development could be a smooth and even process, but it just can't be. Parents and children both need to know that a child's anger can actually be helpful to his* development. The task is to work together to master the frustration or other cause.

Parents need to help the child to use and control his anger instead of allowing it to control him. The process of getting angry can then be used to mobilize his strength instead of disorganizing him. Reading together and discussing this book should prove very helpful. Listening attentively to the child's responses is a vital part of the process.

There are many times along the road to growing up when the parents must intercede. Not everything that catches the child's eye may be handled. There must be some "hands off" rules. Not everything intriguing may be explored. There must be some "stay out" rules. Even though enforcement of these rules elicits an angry response from the child, parents have to stay in charge.

---

*The authors use *he*, *him*, and *his* for simplicity instead of the somewhat awkward *he or she*, *his or her*, and *him or her*, but with no suggestion of preference implied.

There are times for noise and times for quiet, times for running and times for sitting. Very often the child feels that the parents' rules, the parents' "no!" get in his way. The parents' job is to say "no" lovingly, consistently, and firmly when necessary. The rules should be few and not nagging. But rules there must be.

Important rules to be laid down early are those about eating, sleeping, toileting, and respect for other people and their property. Out of this discipline comes growth.

Growth must be allowed to proceed at the child's pace. Not every forward step will be permanent. When the child is tired or frightened, he will often find it comforting to go back to younger behavior. Make allowances for these small regressions. It is the end result that counts, not the speed along the way.

Anger on the child's part, as growing up progresses, must be allowed. It needs always to be understood, but this does not mean that it should always be permitted to run its course unchecked.

At some point in growing up (usually around 3½ years), to hold back and to resist following directions are often signs of emerging independence, and should not be considered solely as defiance. On the other hand, many tasks—such as toilet duties—are now done as gifts the child gives to those he loves and to those he knows love him.

Mastery of new tasks, simple though they may seem to parents, requires real work on the child's part. But if success promises rewards in the form of praise and appreciation, and if help is nearby, the effort will seem worthwhile.

A child learns only gradually that others must be considered important—just as important as he is. He learns that sharing his toys with other children often leads to their sharing their toys with him. But when the going gets difficult—in learning to play with a group, or in learning anything else—anger is usually the first response. Not every child, of course, will react just as the child in the story does; but surely parents will recognize that even as adults they often feel frustrated when they realize that they are not doing something well, or are failing when they really want to succeed.

The child does not enjoy being angry, but at the time it may seem better than feeling sadness or failure. Parents should help the child feel better about himself so that he will give up the anger. Even at this age a child's anger should be treated as an important communication of feeling and should be accorded a warm, though sometimes firm, response.

ROBERT E. SWITZER, M.D.

Former Director of the Children's Division
The Menninger Clinic

J. COTTER HIRSCHBERG, M.D.

William C. Menninger Distinguished Professor of Psychiatry
The Menninger Clinic

Look at me!
I want you to see
I'm growing up.

I'm me,
    me,
    ME!

I feel so good,
I want to say,
"See how strong I am!
Let me have my way!"

If I can't have my way,
if you say "No!"
I may try to kick
or find something to throw.

I don't mean to be bad,

I just want you to see
how great it is
to be me,
me,
ME!

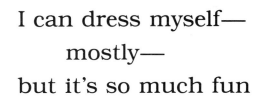

I can dress myself—
mostly—
but it's so much fun

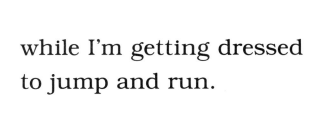

while I'm getting dressed
to jump and run.

I like to find out,
to touch
and explore.

If you won't let me,
I might stamp the floor.

It's hard to keep hands off,
but I think I can.

If you say,
"Don't touch!"
I understand.

I like to shout.

I like to sing.

I like to make noise
with anything.

When grown-ups say,
"Be quiet now!"
sometimes noise seems
to come out anyhow.

Play a quiet game, though,
and you will see
how still-as-a-mouse
I can really be.

I can feed myself
but I like to
                take
                        my
                                time.

Let me try it my way
and we'll get along fine.

If you say,
"Finish that now!"
or "Hurry up!"
I may push my dish
    or tip my cup.

I like to do
the things I should.
In my
own
sweet
time.

I want to be good.

If grown-ups rush me
or act like they're mad,
I often change
    from good to bad.

All by myself
I like to try
to do new things—
but with you close by.

I like to run and hide,
but I want to be
sure that you will come
looking for me.

I like to play with toys—
all the toys I see.
I want them
        WHEN I want them—
and all for ME!

I don't like to give things up.
It's hard to share toys
with other
        little girls and boys.

But they want to play.
They like toys too.
Sometimes I take turns.
"Here's a toy for you."

I'm not so grown-up
that I don't sometimes cry,

but when you are near
my tears are soon dry.

I want to please you,
don't you see,

but I've got to show you
that I'm me,
    me,
    ME!